—The—
Imaginal
Marriage

Books by Eleanor Stanford

The Book of Sleep
Bartram's Garden
The Imaginal Marriage

——The——
Imaginal
Marriage

Eleanor Stanford

Carnegie Mellon University Press
Pittsburgh 2018

ACKNOWLEDGMENTS

Many thanks to the editors of the following journals, where these poems previously appeared:

AGNI Online: "Centralia," "With J., Discussing Grammar in the Anarchist Coffee Shop, West Philadelphia"
Anthropology and Humanism: "Dona França," "Dona Bela, Midwife of Lençóis," "Afterbirth"
Baltimore Review: "November, your metal teeth"
Beloit Poetry Journal: "Devil's Pool," "Romance Sonámbulo"
Berkeley Poetry Review: "Aphasic Sonnet"
Birmingham Poetry Review: "Lepidoptera of the Diamond Highlands"
december: "Late Fall," "Nine-Banded Armadillo"
Denver Quarterly: "Small Towns of Southeastern PA," "Mary-close-the-door"
Colorado Review: "Sombre Hummingbird"
Gettysburg Review: "Ezra Becoming Kosher," "Field Guide to Wild Mushrooms," "Nomenclature"
Harvard Review: "Long-Billed Curlew"
Hotel Amerika: "Folk Medicine," "Dona Bela Recalls Her Seven Husbands"
Poetry Northwest: "Sequelae," "At the Lençóis River"
Prairie Schooner: "Dona Terezinha's Oriole," "The Midwives," "Dona Aúrea," "Dona Orínia's Hyacinth Macaw"
Prism: "My sons taught me"
River Styx: "How Caves Are Formed"
Southwest Review: "Anorexic Sonnet"
Subtropics: "Medical History"

"Long-Billed Curlew" and "Ezra Becoming Kosher" also appeared in *Poetry Daily*.

"Dona França," "Dona Bela, Midwife of Lençóis," and "Afterbirth" won the Ethnographic Poetry Contest from the Society for Humanistic Anthropology.

"Anorexic Sonnet" won the Elizabeth Matchett Stover Award from *Southwest Review*.

Book design by Kate Martin

Library of Congress Control Number 2018935070
ISBN 978-0-88748-641-8
Printed and bound in the United States of America

10 9 8 7 6 5 4 3 2 1

CONTENTS

Wind Gap

INTRODUCTION

Between 2014 and 2016, I spent several months in rural Bahia as a Fulbright fellow, traveling around the countryside and listening to and recording the stories of traditional midwives there.

Mary Lúcia Galvão, a university-trained midwife and tireless advocate for women's reproductive rights, graciously took me under her wing. She fed me and put me up in her spare bedroom and we collaborated on her project to preserve the midwives' histories and their practices. Mary Lúcia is also developing a registry of traditional midwives across the country, but this is a tricky business, as many of these women are in their eighties and nineties, and no longer practicing, and are often reluctant to own the title *parteira*, whether from modesty or fear of discrimination. According to the American midwife and writer Ina May Gaskin—midwifery in Brazil is "in danger of extinction."

Brazil, particularly its economically depressed regions in the North, faces enormous challenges in terms of resources and access to safe birth, with hospitals that are ill-equipped, understaffed, and geographically inaccessible. Meanwhile, in the cities of Rio and São Paulo, the private hospitals have C-section rates as high as 98 or 99 percent, when the World Health Organization recommends a rate of 10 to 15 percent. Midwifery could help alleviate many of these disparities in Brazil, but it's persecuted rather than supported by the government.

Traveling with Mary Lúcia, I spent time with sixteen midwives, and also with their daughters and granddaughters. Mary Lúcia took me to *quilombos* (maroon communities), to Candomblé *terreiros* (sites of worship), and to hidden enclaves in the Atlantic forest and on the Bay of All Saints. We traveled through the interior of the state of Bahia and up the coast into Sergipe. I met not only the midwives, but the women whose babies they'd caught, and those babies themselves, now grown, who refer to the midwives with great affection as their *mães de umbigo*—bellybutton mothers.

Once you enter the world of the midwives, Mary Lúcia told me, *you'll never leave.*

I watched Dona França's ninety-four-year-old hands cutting garlic. I saw Dona Maria's tiny feet in wool socks and child's sandals. I made note of Dona Aúrea's sour countenance as she offered me windfall oranges from her yard and talked earnestly about apocalypse.

I was moved by the midwives' clear-eyed competence and wisdom, as well as their ability to retain their wonder and sense of humor in the face of enormous hardship. And I soon found the midwives' magic seeping into my poems. The midwives taught me to embrace paradox and mystery. As the speaker in one of these poems says, speaking of the body in childbirth, "the same frame that contains us sometimes lets us go." So too with marriage and childrearing. So too with love.

The Brazilian Ministry of Health has pledged to pay traditional midwives the equivalent of ten dollars for each birth they attend, although in reality they are rarely paid in money. They are paid in plucked chickens or crocheted tablecloths, or not at all. Let these poems be an offering, then, too. I bow to these women's fortitude and insight, to their spirit and their sly resourcefulness. To Dona Aúrea, eighty-seven years old, chopping sugar cane with a machete. To Mary Lúcia, giving me her guru's totem to slip into my bra. To Dona Orínia, with a bright green parrot on her shoulder, her voice breaking into tears, then just as quickly into laughter.

Submerged River

Metaphysics

In the dim cantina strung
with little lights, you lifted
my hand to your lips and bit
the fleshy edge. Time
bared its teeth
in the parking meters
on the cold street. Time
condensed: sweat-beaded,
transparent, salty.
Time: that delicacy
from the interior
I'd nibbled once,
the sweet-lobed succulent
also called *palma*.

The fox

who lives behind your suburban twin
browses among the trash cans. Did you believe
you dreamed it? Your son, sidling toward ten,
appearing almost every night now
in your bedroom, dragging his elaborately quilted
fears. Drowning. Divorce. Attacking raccoons.
Tornadoes. His younger brother falling
out the window.

The fox lifts her delicately pointed face
and watches coolly. Once
you held such a subtle mammal
in your arms, stroked its softly furred
crown, wanting only
to burrow into a quiet nest, somewhere
in the debris of your old life.

The fox's large ears are drawn back, listening.
Clever predator. Omnivorous.

Could you have imagined then
that you would long
for this interrupted sleep, for the chance
to take your son's sly limbs into your warm bed,
to let him come to you with hurricane-
strength winds, kidnapping, natural
and unnatural disaster?

Sombre Hummingbird
Capão Valley, Brazil

The Batista waterfall is half-
erased, disappears
before it hits the ground. Dona Aúrea
loves to talk about how
the world is ending. At my ear,
this drab throb, the canyon swallowing
the sun. I hold a glass of cachaça
up to the sinking light: a cloudy
eye. Once when we were young
and unyoked we watched oxen
mill the sugar cane to terrifying
proof. Dona Aúrea, it's true, the world
is ending: in the cataract's
obliterating mist. In the kiss
of the hummingbird's
fringed tongue.

Anorexic Sonnet

I bite
my Life-
saver
in half.
Sugar
a knife,
hunger-
honed, grief-
sharpened.
My mouth's
pale arc
afloat.
It's dark.
There is
no boat.

Ezra Becoming Kosher

What's memory but a shucked oyster,
salt-rimed and shivering?

       At one and a half,
he pointed at the ceiling fan, said
rotate, as though his mouth was origin
of some first turning.

So many rules to be a Jew,
my mother sighs, leaving behind
Long Island, Flatbush, Yiddishkeit.

Ezra, balanced between the past
and a tender pork roast, puts down
his fork.

What's memory but an omnivorous
shadow, cloven-hoofed?

Whose memory? Not mine.

Between what my mother won't cop to,
and what my son won't eat, I'm half-invisible,
half-confused.

       Already, at nine, he retreats behind his too-long
bangs and Bach inventions.

And my mother, the hard bead of Ashkenazi
irony cut out of her left breast, radiated, her Judaism, too,
now in full remission.

Memory, relentless bottom-feeder,
gatherer of refuse and debris—

                    And Ezra, turning
away, knowing: thou shalt not cook the kid
in its mother's milk; the animal should be bled
swiftly and just so, prayers said thus
over its bowed head.

Aphasic Sonnet

My son's first word was in another tongue.
Quer: un-conjugated want. He held
hibiscus flowers by their throats, pulled
out their pollen-furred demurrals, and flung

them speechless in the pool. *Quer*: he clung
to me, the light at five a.m. a still
meniscus, hovering, about to spill.
Subjectless, his want a flame tree hung

with blazing verbs. In another hemisphere,
my grandmother reached for words, her English
suddenly deciduous. My son's *quer*,
her stutter--each a question, quest, a list
of grievances. Also a kind of prayer.
The root of utterance longing for what's missed.

Medical History

When did the pain start?
Three weeks ago, Saturday.
Deep breath.
It comes and goes.
When did the pain—
It started with my mother.
When?
In 1979, the gray skies of São Paulo, summer a hammered
metal helmet.
I'm sorry. My hands are cold. Again?
In Bavaria, before I was born, when my grandfather held
the four tasseled corners of the world in his hand and
prayed.
Other side.
In a lacquer factory in Hokkaido: the gloss, the stink, the
smooth reflective surface.
When?
1934. 1968. When I was five, and learned to move from one
element to another. Water to air. Dark to—
The pain?
Stabbing. Dull. A branch extending from—
Higher?
Lower.
The pain?
Yes. A tight-stitched shawl. A lacquer bowl—
Here? Where the stomach—
burnished vessel,
meets the ileum.
Ornamental thread I don't believe in.
Tender?
Yes.

Long-Billed Curlew (*Numenius longistrosis*)

Would it help to know that God
is no relation etymologically
to good?

But closer to pour, to cast,
to funnel?

Dark above,
paler below:

the wing linings visible
in flight.

Closer to the name
invoked, the call
loud and musical, ascending.

One-Room Cabin
Capão Valley, Brazil

Its many rooms: pressure cooker on the stove,
its little hat set spinning. Net draping the bed,
full of holes, that trapped
the needle's charged hum at my ear
all night. Corners and eaves. Ten elbows,
ten knees. Five hearts, each walled off
into cavernous ventricles, high-ceilinged atria.
The toilet that flushed into the root system
of the banana tree outside. Circular room of feathers
and bent twigs our boys made. Glowing room
you slipped into after I was asleep,
where you met your lover and whispered
with electric tongues. Room of the mountains,
room of the wind. Room where the birds
woke me each morning at five. The one
called Washerwoman, the one called
Suffering. The colorful and tragic
singers whose songs
ushered me through doors
into rooms I didn't know
were there, the house always bigger
than you think and full of secrets.

November, your metal teeth

shine all night. The harmonica's unspeakable
wheeze, brace at his neck as though
he'd been in a terrible
accident. November, our boys
learned to play hearts. I heard them muttering
to each other: *Where's the bad lady?* and
*You can't play hearts until hearts
have been broken.* Maybe
you could just say the one word,
the therapist said. Just the one. *You.*
But he couldn't.
November, I painted my fingernails
black. November, I stood on one leg
in yoga class and cried.
Thanksgiving, I drank too much wine
and tried to disappear. There was another ship, not
the Mayflower, our son said, and that one sank,
and all the people died. Under the covers, the boys
showed their hands. *You're bleeding,*
they said. *Hearts have been broken,*
they reminded each other. November,
your moon bends around me, a bright
and limber harmonica, full of teeth.
A thin letter, undeliverable. *You.*

Dona Aúrea

I was midwife
to fear. Its
crowning. Its bloody
show. Midwife
to sun opening
the cervix of
the valley,
slipping through
the narrow pass
to Angêlica Falls.
I was midwife to
spirit and to form.
To the smooth
egg still warm
from the chicken.
Midwife to death,
too. The wind
astonishing the canyon.
Shaking
that overtakes
a body in transition.
There was
no other.
When they called
me I came.

Lepidoptera of the Diamond Highlands
Capão Valley, Brazil

Set against the canyon's
serrated jaw,
in the mosquito net's
silver filaments, we spun
an imaginal marriage. *Some build*
an escape hatch. Others have spines
with which they can cut
or tear their way out. But how
to turn this liquefied
self into something you could call
adult? How to reassemble
our old organs into
claspers, a long sucking
tube, a pair of compound eyes?

How Caves Are Formed
Lençóis, Bahia

Small cracks marry
below the surface,
then deepen: a slow
wearing away.

The making
of our stony
wedding cake:

Sometimes a desert,
sometimes a shallow
sea.

The wall a cool
back arched against
your hand.

When I couldn't eat
I could at least
gloat at bone
and hollow.

Mouth of the submerged
river, so clear
that visitors walk into it
still wearing their shoes.

The Interior

Mary-close-the-door

The dusty purple flower
speckles the roadside
in the interior, its bloom
a hinged ingress
that flinches at the lightest
touch--even the sun's
rough hand; even
the wind. Mary Lúcia,
why didn't I listen
when you told me
to take a lover
I could leave behind
in Maragogipe?
Why didn't I
shut like that
under his touch?
Why allow myself
to open further?
In Spanish, it's called
moriviví: I died; I lived.
In English, shameplant.

Dona Terezinha's Oriole

The cage swings above
cow pasture. Wind
through the tree branches,
and bars of light and dark
shifting on the hard-trod
ground. Even the beams
of your own body are meant
to open. You don't
believe me? Terezinha's
seen: ribs unhinge; hips
pivot. The same frame
that contains us sometimes
lets us go. Are you surprised?
But it's the midwife's job
to bring suffering into the world
as well as beauty. Sofrê,
they call me. Do you think
that these sweet syllables
mean grief? She reaches
her bent finger
through the bars
to touch my bright
cupped flame.

At the Lençóis River
Bahia, Brazil

A green snake
slips between the rocks.
Green of mango leaves, green
of lost chances.

Thank God for work,
for pounding clothes
against the sandstone.
For heft and scrub, wet
sheet twisted like an asp.

The past slithers
from that crevasse—
flickering, silent, mostly
harmless.

Who lives without
regret? Maybe
the snake, leaving behind
her skin like so many shimmering
cocktail dresses.

Her bite sets your mouth
buzzing, your blood electric
with remorse. It's not
fatal, only briefly
makes you
wish you were dead.

Introduction to the Book of the Midwife

We thought of the book as though
we were pregnant, preparing for a normal healthy birth.

The baby was born: here it is!

We thought of the book as something that could accompany
the midwife: an amulet, a prayer, a ribbon from the church of Bomfim
she could tie around her wrist.

We thought of the book as full of pictures, for those midwives
who have not yet learned to read and write.

We thought of the book as a way of remembering.

We thought of the book as an answer to questions
she didn't know yet that she had.

Dona Maria
Amapá, Brazil

Over the black waters of the Anapu pass
woodcutters' boats, trawlers from the Secretary
of Health. Past the hidden banks of Laranjal,
a raft of names and unfamiliar rules. *My poor*
son, so small and having to work with his body
in the water, harvesting hearts of palm.
Over the Anapu's black current:
yellow fever, fantastic winged fish.
Underneath: alligators,
inexplicable shipwrecks. *Sister,*
there are leeches there, and he's so skinny
I'd like to be a bird, so at lunchtime
I could bring his food to him.

The Lying-In

The grandmothers come
with dishcloth-swaddled pots
of bone soup, jars of cachaça steeped
in honey. And their lists
of prohibitions: no beef
or capybara. No limes or sour
oranges. No remorse to pucker the mouth
like umbú fruit. You're a mother now:
factory of milk and guilt. If you're not
careful, your breasts will turn
to stone. Let the baby drink.
Express the excess
in the sink.

The Midwives
Bahia, Brazil

The secrets of philosophy
are the secrets of the body.

You think because we're old and wear headscarves
and lay our hands on pregnant bellies
we don't know how the baby got in there?

You think we didn't once, or many times, slink
into the thicket at the edge of town
with a man, or even by ourselves?

The secrets of the body
are deeper.

You think we didn't once or twice invite
the delivery boy in for a quick fuck?

Dona Bela, Midwife of Lençóis
Bahia, Brazil

1.

She made her way across hunger and thirst
She grew in the forest of the twentieth century
She ate cactus, leaf and fruit
With her hands she rubbed the belly
Rubbed amulet, trough, the knot umbilical
The science of birth belonged to Dona Bela
Bath of cashew husk and umburana bark
She caught one thousand one hundred and twenty babies
Dona Bela danced samba with Sutão of the Forest
And wheeled over the Capivara River
like a hawk
Of seven husbands she was the lover

2.

She lost her mother in childbirth
She left her people to become
midwife of the dirt roads and the cities.
Nanã the Earth goddess taught her the art
of catching babies. Curious Dona Bela: her plate
was the vast tablelands. Her cup
the curved frond of a bromeliad.

Snake, Dona Bela said, when she meant
clothesline.
Savior, she said, meaning
voice recorder.

The frill of lichens her lace collar.
The candombá lily a green ribbon for her hair.

3.

The *barbeiros* in her mud walls
kissed her while she slept.
Then neither Jesus nor her orixás
could unclasp the crochet hooks
in her blood.

Her heart a patchwork
of holes, its muscles worn thin
as bobbin lace.

Dona Bela: daughter
of the earth goddess Nanā,
mother of Julita made
of cloth.

One thousand one hundred
and twenty times her hands
had touched the scrap of ripped
caul, pulled back
its pale spiderweb.

Now those hands wove another: the blue
of seven lovers, blue dress of a saint's
daughter, blue of her diamond-
scarred Sincorá Mountains
at sundown.

In this fine shroud of sky
was she buried.

Dona França
Conceição dos Gatos, Brazil

Boys develop sooner
in the womb. It's true.
I've held a three-months
fetus, already a little
man. Daughter, where's
my thimbleful
of coffee?
The girls—they're
still half-
fish. Less willing
to commit. Isn't it
so, daughter?
Sugar, yes.
And milk.

Footling

Nothing would make
you turn: not prayer,
or baths of sword
mango, not lying
upside down. The rest
of the world spun. Not
you. Not even
the midwife's hands,
pushing the immovable
mountain
while I groaned.

But the hills: abrupt
knobs of limestone
arising from an ancient
seabed. It's almost enough
to make me believe
in another possible
world, one into which
you rush, smooth water
through a narrow
flue. A world
built not on rupture
but on a gentle
accretion or
wearing away.

Dona Orínia's Hyacinth Macaw
Baxíos, Sergipe, Brazil

How tenderly she'd pinion me:
my heart a small throb beneath
her thumb. For years this went on:
the Spanish came and went, bought up
the coastline, paid in bad credit.
Their fancy hotels ill-
conceived, part-built, like the son
she never stopped mourning,
the boy born still
amphibious. One can live an entire life
in the shallows. The ocean
murky-eyed like us; like us,
flightless, spreading
its gray wing. With firm
and steady hands, she'd apply
the styptic powder
to staunch the blood.

Introduction to the Book of the Midwife

Many Brazilians, including the authors
themselves, were born
                      with the help of midwives.
But we also know that, alone,
the midwives cannot resolve the most difficult
cases:
              breech, hemorrhage, broken spirit,
                              evil eye.

Dona Bela Recalls Her Seven Husbands
Chapada Diamantina, Brazil

1. Swift lizard, sunning under a rock ledge.
2. My interior: crooked jackfruit tree, dirt road out of my childhood.
3. His hands on my body, undoing the latches.
4. To manage thriftily.
5. Only one I wed in a church. A wager with God, the laughable odds.
6. Sundays panning in the river, gravel and grit, and nothing to show.
7. Glittering-throated emerald. Amethyst woodstar. Winged shimmer—endemic, uncatchable.

Folk Medicine

The midwives say: the body is also
a door. Open, closed—

For toothache, prayer
and a mango-leaf bath.

For shingles, call on the vermin—
the lizard, the spider, the snake.

I'll tell you a story, the midwives say.
The fire creaking on hinges
of piauí bark. All true.

The fish smoking a cigarette.
Manioc root snaking
from here to Salvador.

Porridge of the souls
to close the portal.

All true: the shack in the Atlantic
forest, wind in the banana leaves.

Dog porridge. Porridge
of Santo António.

The midwives singing,
singing, and the teenage girls
staring into their glowing cells.

His hand on the ends
of my hair. Asking: is it
real? The little boats in the harbor
far below.

For snakebite: Prayer.
Infusion of lemon balm.

All true: I'll build you a house,
he said, a little house,
if you stay.

The midwives say: The birds
are falling. The planets
all in disarray.

Translation's a door, too—

The talking donkeys. The mother
who eats a chunk of flesh
from the daughter's thigh—

A trapdoor.

The first preventative is not
saying the name of the sickness.

Real, not real, and his hands
opening a room without
a door.

The second: once established,
not to let it spread.

If you're able, express the gall
over the bite.

Dilation

The moon
floating in the icy water
of the bitter river

The two centimeters
between unbearable
and born

Introduction to the Book of the Midwife

In the dense forests of the interior,
in this universe of little rivers,
the body holds no mysteries.

Even children observe births,
stroke the foreheads of laboring women,
are sent to toss out the placenta.

In exchange for her labor, the midwife
receives: a tambourine of flour, an ear
of corn, a plucked chicken.

Nine-Banded Armadillo (*Dacypsus novemcintus*)
Capão Valley, Brazil

Night digs up the ravine
with her large claws. Her omnivorous
snout and sudden toothless grief.

Mother, please note my new address: House
with the Enormous Jackfruit Tree,
In the Forest. You can write to me
care of the general store
on Circus Road, care of
the banana grove.

Mother, my daughter emerged
into a different century than I did: a shifting
of bony plates, tectonic groan.

Care of the crooked peaks
of the Sincorá mountains,
of the peculiar articulations
of her spine.

Mother, how did you watch me
ride my bicycle away from Santa Catarina,
teetering with a six-months pregnant belly,
and not roll up into a ball
right there on the side of the road?

Please write to me, Mother, and tell me
how: care of the riverbed,
care of the armored ridges,
of this Pleistocene dark.

Afterbirth
Dona Terezinha (Corte Grande, Bahia)

Where I come from's nothing
but a wide gash in the Atlantic
forest. When I was fifteen
I married. When I was twenty,
I lost my fourth child
to fever. *Parteira*, the women
called me, as though
I did something other
than wait with them
through inevitable
pain. For twenty years
he slept with a machete
beneath his pillow. When I woke
to attend a birth,
he wielded it. When I spoke
too loud, or broke
something, or when cachaça burned
an unbearable hole in his chest, the knife
came out. *Parteira*, he called me,
his voice flat and sharp
as the blade through cane's
knuckles. Then each fleshy fingertip
slipped off, a placenta
un-attaching itself.

Sequelae

What follows from love
is grief. Do you think
you've found another way?

Look at the young man
in the corner, his face
twisted, his voice
the bark of a dog.

Do you think
his mother conceived,
in any green shudder
of the Atlantic forest,
such rocky scarps?

Do you think she doesn't
long still, every day,
to be delivered?

Wind Gap

Devil's Pool
Wissahickon Creek, Philadelphia

In the middle of my life,
a rift:

gap of still water. Schist cool
against my back, and my body
burning.

In the middle of my life,
a clearing:

mica-flecked ache. A ledge
to jump off.

Longing's metamorphic, too—
a deep fault,
geologic.

All I want is something
to plunge me into the cold
current.

Someone to pull me
out, lichen-slick, sputtering.

Centralia

In candlelit flickering, you trace
my ribs' uneven seams.
Not far from here, a town
built on a mine caught fire
fifty years ago and is still
burning. Beneath the overburden
of those other lives—friable surface
where residents of small hope
and coal smoke make peanut butter
sandwiches or bicker, or sing
their coal-tinged lullabies—we move
in upcast shadow. Lampless
and luminous, breath crumbles again
in the smoldering, the bitumen,
the glittering ore body.

With J., Discussing Grammar in the Anarchist Coffee Shop, West Philadelphia

There is only one kind
of sentence, you insist:
declarative. Meaning,
when you ask—our hands
conjugating each other
across the table—do you
love me, what you are saying
is *you love me*. Meaning,
the basic unit can only be
affirmative: soft
gray rain fogging
the glass. Palm
on palm. Black coffee
in a small tin cup.

Lovesick and sleepless, I recite the curandeira's advice

For an open chest, only prayer. For suppurating
wounds, tail of a smoked porcupine, or

vulture feather. For itch,
bath of mastic. For catarrh,

sweet broom, crushed
with milk. For the heart,

tea of washed blood.

Mary Lúcia, from her garden in Itaparica, 7,000 kilometers away, diagnoses me

Amor, it's good to hear you're feeling
better, but listen: you know sickness in the throat's
a sign of that which we can't speak
or feel.

         My dear, if you were here, I'd heat you a bath
of chamomile. Or we'd sit in the sand
with an ice-cold beer.

            I'd sequester you in my witch's kitchen,
feed you fish moqueca and manioc cake
until your tongue turned soft as tapioca,
and secrets scattered like so many seashells
on the tile floor.

Honey, I've sat with enough laboring women to know
the body clamps shut when the throat can't let go.

Best to ask yourself, querida, what are you swallowing,
guzzling, bottling up?

            It must be so cold there, querida,
but you know my advice for all ailments: appeal
to the forces of light, and always swim, naked if possible,
in whatever body of water presents itself.

Small Towns of Southeastern PA

Between us, pine
and estuary. Between us,
the silt-tongued Lehigh.
Bird-in-hand. Flying hills.
Three Mile Island.
Dream-plant where
atoms of meaning
decay and recombine.
Between us, seven
valleys. Shale, source
rock. Furnace Creek.
Between us: screeching
and teeth. Salt-edged
heat. Errata etched
in belly's shallow dip.
Between us, hip
and hip: anthracite, wind gap,
flash flood.

My sons taught me

to kiss the ball
with my laces.
Taught me
look up, aim
straight, follow
through. I moved
with no finesse
whatsoever
from that life
to this, this
love to that:
leaving my lover's
bed to collide
with their small
bodies on the field
where we met
as unknowable
opponents, not
as ones who'd grown
from the cells
of the other's
body. Patient
and full of their own
knowledge
my sons showed me
pass and deflect,
one touch, give
and go.

Pennsylvania Turnpike

Winter-honed knife, halving
the space between us.
Each week, the having
and not having. And in the fields
beside the road, the calving.

Romance Sonámbulo

On the Línea Verde north
of Salvador the rain comes
hard and swift. Then
disappears. For so long
you didn't
exist: I was
happy or sad, but
my tears had nothing to do
with you. I ate lobster
in Jacuipe with Mary Lúcia, licked
olho alho from my fingers and
didn't think of you
in a cornfield
in Pennsylvania,
in Barcelona or
Jersey City or
L.A. It was my words
that brought you
to me, and my words
that will one day
send you away. That's
how it is, Mary Lúcia
says, shaking
her head at my foolishness
and the rain
green over the water.

Nomenclature

If we were a species,
it would be something
iridescent,
brief lived, many
limbed. After mating,
the segmented
body, mouth-parts
recalibrating. Your voice
in my ear, translating
Aristotle's weakness
of will. After Aristotle,
coffee and yogurt
with honey. Then
swimming in the cold
creek. After shivering,
sun on a warm rock.
After kissing, the naming
of the plants
and animals: family,
order, genus, species.
How to preserve
in words the pale ache
of new leaves?
Deciduous, I said—like
teeth. Your tongue,
latinate, elaborate,
in my mouth.

Trenton: Late May, Early Evening

We step out of the train station: warm
air, smell of burning trash
and Queen Anne's lace wilting
through the hurricane fence.

My students never want to say
the words they really mean. *Little singers*,
they write, instead of birds.

In a bodega, we find a jar of something tentacled
preserved in brine. Plant or animal? Root or stalk?

The sun is going down behind an overpass.
Retracting the day, as Chaucer, at the end of his life,
tried to take it all back.

As they say in Cataluña

With you, tuna fish
and day-old rice.
With you, borrowed
rooms, salt
constellating
our skin.
With you, summer
star, evening star,
banjo's incandescent
body, and
the seventeen thousand
other planets—
all the shapes intelligent
life might take: galaxy
of bread crumbs,
green-blooming
allium. Celestial
leavening, translucent
riddle of skin
within skin.

September

I'm fragile as the garlic's paper dress.
I haven't slept, and driving here I crashed
the car. Not hurt, but shaken, I let
you gather me, stroke my disheveled

hair. Unpeel my sweat-damp shirt, unzip
my skirt. Beneath the skin, I'm that smooth,
that pointed. The heart splits, but each rib
can grow another whole. That's what I choose

to tell myself, my sons and husband elsewhere,
my life deep-riven. Silverskin.
Mother-of-pearl. We'll rise from bed at dusk, pare
each clove, arterial, and bury it in

earth. And hope the bulb is winter-hardy, disposed to
sprout among the roots of wilting cosmos.

Late Fall

Hum of sun on limestone,
hymn of tongue and thrum
of all the sonorants
unsaid: of palm and limb,
of sky breathing us in
its one continuant
blue lung. In my mouth
sound's fled.
All around, instead,
drought-softened grass
that bends
to kiss the ground.

You Know How to Love at a Distance

Your daughter, tender ocotillo,
blazes in the dry heat
of a distant desert
Sometimes she appears
impervious, her needs
spreading their shallow
roots outward sometimes
she opens her mouth around
the little camera as though
to swallow you

I have taken to smoking a cigarette
at two in the afternoon just
so I can make my longing
visible, my day empty
of you, and the sky, clear and full
of March wind

With Mary Lúcia and Luciana in Maragogipe
Bahia, Brazil

It rained, the boat never came,
the general store was sold out
of corn cakes and Yemanjá statues. Instead
we took shelter under a torn
awning, drank beer and cracked the shells
of small crabs, dipped them
in peppery manioc paste. In our minds
we bought a small plot
of land, planted banana trees
and sweet potatoes, we tilled
and harvested, my sons grew
lithe and wild, gathering crustaceans
from the mangrove roots. Luciana left
her various loves in various cities
and learned the secrets
of the midwives from you, and you
left your stark apartment and your sadnesses
in Salvador, hours away by raft
on the slow-moving Paraguaçu River.
After an hour the sun came out
but we were glad by then the boatman
hadn't come. If he had we'd never
have lived this entire life—
never have seen the procession
of drums and lilies in honor of Oxum,
every Friday a different god, never
have felt our feet in the mud finer
than silk slippers, never have met
María Eduarda, age four, glossy pigtails
and eyes like dark water, tucking a flower
behind her ear, and each of us leaning
toward her also to be so blessed.

Outside a Dress Shop

We sit on stone steps,
under the mannequin's
headless gaze, while
in the back room

a woman with a mouthful
of pins tacks hems
with precision I'll never
have. Remember,

you said, the boat
from Fogo to Brava,
and how we watched one woman
nurse another's baby,

still young enough then
to believe we knew how
love worked, its patterns
and hidden seams, or

if not, we would
soon, the spray off the Atlantic
stitching itself
to our skin.

Solstice

Let's have another, I murmur,
the ice in my glass
melting, mandolin a twinge
in my ribcage and the fire dying
in the fire pit. You listen
to our son singing, his voice
not yet broken, not yet set.
Some bright morning
when this life is over, I'll—
in the almost dark,
June's beneficence
endless—*fly away, like a bird*
June's brinksmanship steep,
from these prison walls
I'll fly, I'll—and no,
you shake your head,
no more, the light
fading, brimming briefly
on the peony's cheek.

Field Guide to Wild Mushrooms

1. Spring

Some mushrooms are orphans.
Neither gilled nor pored; inky, glistening, uncertain.
This is not a beginner's mushroom.

2. Summer

How far back can your memory reach?

Near heavily traveled roads; turning yellow when bruised
from handling; in grassy places, alone; in arcs
and circles.

Giant polypore, blackening polypore—
in incandescent light, single or scattered, depressed
at the stem.

Save the tough parts
to boil for soup.

3. Fall

It's not decay, but
a natural
self-digesting

no matter what the old guidebooks say—man
on horseback, canary—

Perhaps in the distant past,
equestrians wore yellow hats.

4. Winter

Moon melon, velvet foot, late oyster:

All of our mistakes
have been edible.

We Should Always Remember the Unforeseen Can Happen

In the middle of the road it might begin to rain.
The road might be in bad condition, and even a cart unable to pass.
If there is a car, it can run out of gas, or pop a tire.
If there is a boat, its motor might not start.

Sometimes the only way is to carry the woman in a hammock.

And still, after all this, arriving at the hospital, it can happen
that the maternity ward is full, and the baby will come
as it would have—in the road, in the mud, in the boat—slipping
into whatever hands are there to receive it.

Dan: always, without whom none of this is possible.

Meu coração, luz da minha vida: Ezra, Ruben, and Joaquin.

Jeff: for showing me so many possible worlds I didn't know existed.

Mary Lúcia Galvão: Amiga, comadre, irmã. Por compartilhar comigo a sua generosidade, beleza, espírito e força, e o axé da Bahia. Obrigada nem chega.

The midwives: Dona Aúrea, Dona França, Dona Vanilda, Dona Terezinha, Dr. Aúreo, Natália, Marilanda Lima, Ina May Gaskin, Christy Santoro, and all the others, in Brazil and elsewhere, who give so much of themselves, often without recompense or recognition. Amor e graditão.

My teachers: Lisa Russ-Spaar, Rita Dove, Charles Wright, Greg Orr.

The rest of my family and friends: Mom and Dad, Isaac, George, Sam, Nikole, Michelle, Sonia, Shotaro, Michelle, Brett, Viv, Ted and all the nieces and nephews. Jessica Lee, Laura Rizzo, Kim Lipetz, Rebecca Benarroch, Jessica Broome, Jenny Smith, Diane Wohland, Jen Callaghan, Ashley Minihan.

Nabeel, for finding me.

Thank you to Sarah Blake for reading and feedback, weekly poetry hangouts and much more.

Thank you to the Fulbright foundation, for supporting this project.

Many thanks to Jerry, Cynthia, Connie, and Carnegie Mellon University Press.

And in memoriam: my beloved grandparents, Rita and Abe Hazelcorn.